IT'S TIME TO EAT A DRAGON FRUIT

It's Time to Eat a Dragon Fruit

Walter the Educator

Silent King Books
A WhichHead Entertainment Imprint

Copyright © 2024 by Walter the Educator

All rights reserved. No part of this book may be reproduced in any manner whatsoever without written per- mission except in the case of brief quotations embodied in critical articles and reviews.

First Printing, 2024

Disclaimer

This book is a literary work; the story is not about specific persons, locations, situations, and/or circumstances unless mentioned in a historical context. Any resemblance to real persons, locations, situations, and/or circumstances is coincidental. This book is for entertainment and informational purposes only. The author and publisher offer this information without warranties expressed or implied. No matter the grounds, neither the author nor the publisher will be accountable for any losses, injuries, or other damages caused by the reader's use of this book. The use of this book acknowledges an understanding and acceptance of this disclaimer.

It's Time to Eat a Dragon Fruit is a collectible early learning book by Walter the Educator suitable for all ages belonging to Walter the Educator's Time to Eat Book Series. Collect more books at WaltertheEducator.com

USE THE EXTRA SPACE TO TAKE NOTES AND DOCUMENT YOUR MEMORIES

DRAGON FRUIT

It's time to eat, what's this I see?

It's Time to Eat a Dragon Fruit

A dragon fruit waiting just for me!

With scaly skin, pink and bright,

It looks like magic, what a sight!

From faraway lands where the dragons play,

This fruit grows strong in a sunny way.

It's bold and bright, like a dragon's flame,

And "dragon fruit" is its mighty name!

Oh, dragon fruit, pink and sweet,

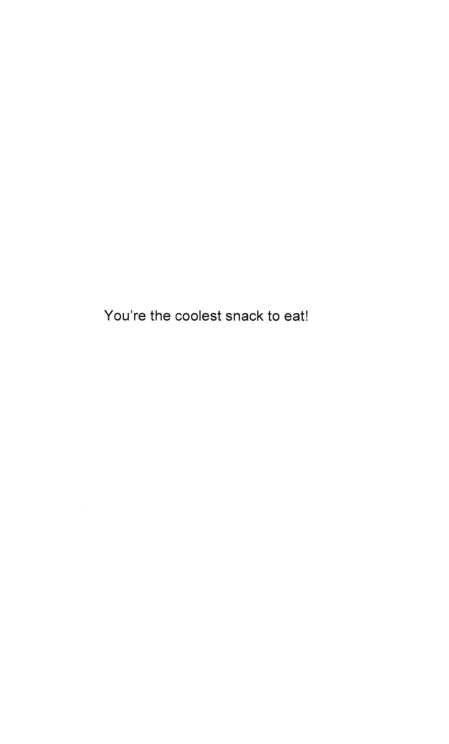

You're the coolest snack to eat!

Bright and fun, with spots of black,

Dragon fruit, I'll be right back!

I slice you open, what's inside?

A white surprise I cannot hide!

Full of tiny seeds, black and neat,

Dragon fruit, you're a special treat!

It's Time to Eat a Dragon Fruit

I take a bite, so cool and fresh,

Soft and juicy, with every mesh.

You taste like honey, light and mild,

Dragon fruit, you make me smile!

Oh, dragon fruit, pink and sweet,

You're the coolest snack to eat!

Bright and fun, with spots of black,

Your skin is spiky, like a dragon's scales,

But inside, the softness never fails!

You're smooth and creamy, full of delight,

A dragon fruit's magic takes flight!

Sometimes you're white, sometimes you're red,

With every color, you fill my head.

With fun ideas and tasty joy,

Dragon fruit is perfect for every girl and boy!

I love your seeds, they add some crunch,

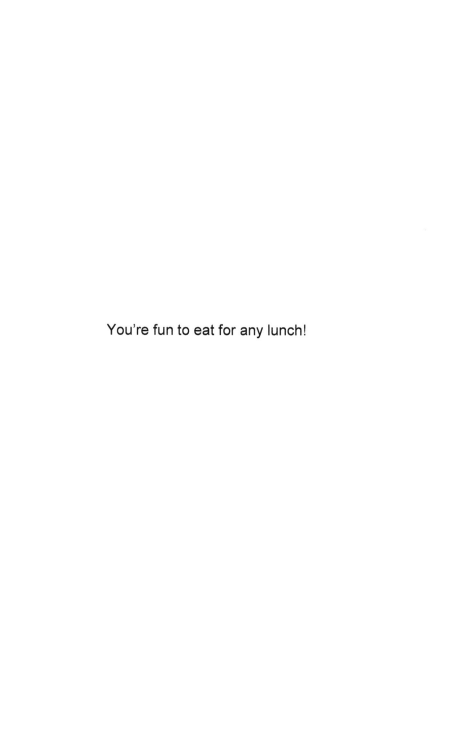

In smoothies or slices, you're always fun,

It's Time to Eat a
Dragon Fruit

Dragon fruit, you're number one!

Oh, dragon fruit, pink and sweet,

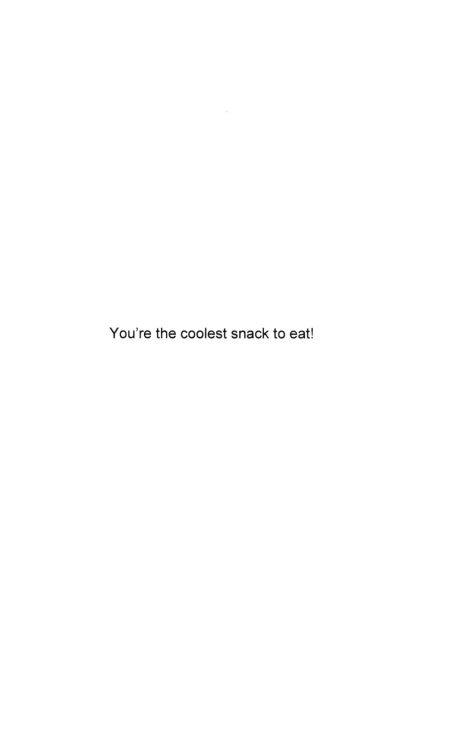
You're the coolest snack to eat!

Bright and fun, with spots of black,

Dragon fruit, I'll be right back!

ABOUT THE CREATOR

Walter the Educator is one of the pseudonyms for Walter Anderson. Formally educated in Chemistry, Business, and Education, he is an educator, an author, a diverse entrepreneur, and he is the son of a disabled war veteran. "Walter the Educator" shares his time between educating and creating. He holds interests and owns several creative projects that entertain, enlighten, enhance, and educate, hoping to inspire and motivate you. Follow, find new works, and stay up to date with Walter the Educator™ at WaltertheEducator.com

Milton Keynes UK
Ingram Content Group UK Ltd.
UKHW021938281024
450365UK00018B/1147